AF344258

# Seattle Sacred Spaces

## and Other Places to Heal the Earth

## B. LEES

PEANUT BUTTER PUBLISHING

Seattle, Washington
Portland, Oregon
Denver, Colorado
Vancouver, B.C.

01.0086


Cover design: David Marty

Typesetting: Packard Productions


Frist printing: August, 1996

10  9  8  7  6  5  4  3  2  1


Published by

Peanut Butter Publishing
226 Second Avenue West
Seattle, Washington  98119
(206) 281-5965

# Contents

To Carolyn Moore
and
Nona Fisher

# Acknowledgments

To me, the word acknowledgment suggests an award recipient on TV trying to thank everyone in a few seconds. I have a page. A parade of people have touched my life:

June, Alfred, Jo Anne, Ron, Patricia, Robert, Susan, Virginia, William, Gene, Tiffany, Tim, Robert, Sara, Anthony, Jon, Antonio, Shannon, Ernest, James, Irene, Elsie, Lola, Karl, Barbara, Don, Elliott, Linda, David, all of those at Saturday School and Central, The YWCA ladies in and out of the pool, and friends at Center Park.

The above are some of the living. I hope those who have gone on form angelic cheering sections for us left behind. I'm going to need a lot more help.

Thanks be to God!

Every part of this earth is sacred:
Every shining pine needle, every sandy shore,
Every mist in the dark woods,
Every clearing and humming insect is holy.
The rocky crest, the Juices of the meadow, the
        beasts and all the people,
All belong to the same family.
Teach your children that earth is our mother;
Whatever befalls the earth befalls the children
        of the earth.
The water's murmur is the voice of our
        father's father.
We are part of the earth and the earth is part of us.
This we know: the earth does not belong to us.
We belong to the earth.
This we know: all things are connected, like the
        blood that unites one family.
All things are connected.
Our God is the same God, whose compassion
        is equal for all.
For we did not weave the web of life; we are
        merely strands within it.
Whatever we do to the web—we do to ourselves.


(adapted from a letter of Chief Sealth, 1854)

# Chapter I
# The Beginning


Hawaii, 1992. Back then, I believed aloha from those beautiful islands  could radiate out to the Pacific rim and on around the world....

Hawaii wasn't ready.

At the YWCA on the windward side of Oahu there was a young Caucasian  woman who saw spiritually in old Hawaiian ways. I had been searching for the mystical beauty understood best by the tutu wahines, only this woman was too young to be a grandmother. Yet we will not forget the time we spent with her.

She told us that the lei was a circle of aloha. It began with the gathering of materials. Leis can be made of flowers, leaves, seeds, shells, nuts and combinations of such. After the gathering, the circle is lovingly made with the recipient in mind.  Then the lei is usually presented with a kiss on each cheek of the receiver.... This is the kind of caring we need.

The woman, Carolyn, Nona and I made a small circle. Nona was in her wheel chair. The rest of us sat on the dry earth. Because the place reached from the mountains to the sea—it was sacred.

We were silent. The birds were not. The trade wind rustled leaves.

The woman chanted. We tried to repeat the words. Hawaiian is not easily repeated. I thought there was something there that could save the world. Nona almost fell asleep. She usually is uptight.

The modern Hawaiian,  almost always a mixture of several races, doesn't seem to want to seek solace or share aloha. S/he wants everyone else, even those born in the islands to feel like outsiders. Hawaiians think of themselves as victims. They blame those who discovered the islands after they did for the decrease of their population and honor one who turned rivers red with blood and who caused bodies to pile beneath Peli Ridge. He united the islands into his kingdom.

There had been a closeness of Hawaiians and nature. Spiritual things were often to be feared. A gap existed between the Alii and the common people. Do all of those, today, who long to go back, think they would be Aliis? In Hawaii today, no one is told they can't eat bananas or pork. It takes more than a shadow to condemn a person to death.

Where has aloha gone?


I came back to Seattle looking for sacred spaces. Perhaps caring from this city, surrounded by mountains and bodies of water, could send meaningful vibrations around the world.

I typed on a small piece of paper, "A Sacred Space to Heal the Earth". I taped it onto my front door.

My search for sacred spaces would begin at home. It should begin within the heart of me.

My friend Carolyn was forty-something. She spent most of her life at the desk of the Health and Fitness program in Seattle's downtown YWCA. Nona and I met her when she was a life guard and we had come swimming.

My friend Nona would be normal if she had been born by Cesarean section. She would have been different. A rough struggle through a birth canal, too small, left her brain damaged. Had she been normal, I might never have found her. As it was, an accident brought me to Center Park where Nona was living in 1975. I had been severely injured. The doctors had said I might never walk again.

I did walk, again. I have shared a good part of my life with those who couldn't.

My motivation was not totally noble. I hated jobs where I sold myself to a business for eight hours a day. Caring for the physically challenged was something like being paid for doing things I had done for a husband and four children. The pay was only a little better, but caring for one person would leave some time for writing. That was the plan.

Center Park is unique. Each disabled person has an apartment. The units were designed so that residents can care for themselves from wheel chairs. To live as independently as possible, some need a few hours of help a week. Some, that much per day. There are a few who require live-in aides.

The person who was responsible for bringing me to Center Park, after my accident, had shared a hospital room with me for a few days. I helped her and others. Finally, Nona asked me to be her live-in aide.

By 1992, when I declared my home a sacred space,

things had gotten complicated. I stayed in Nona's apartment five nights a week. On weekends I could come home. Life was not easy. I was trying to run two households.

On weekday afternoons, I hired some one to care for Nona's needs so that I could come home then, too. I was past retirement age. Coming to my sacred space, I flopped onto my feather bed and took a nap. Getting Nona from bed to chair etc. was physical labor. She has only limited use of her legs. Taking care of Nona and her apartment left little energy to care for my small sea-green house. My ambition to save the world was suffering, too.

My house filled with stacks of papers. I was amazed how many organizations needed my money to help their good causes. I saved magazines with articles I might need some-day. I kept buying books. I didn't have the energy to recycle and organize. I loved my little house and it bothered me that it didn't show. It needed more tender loving care. Instead it was my place of refuge. It was taking care of me.

Each month a social security payment was placed, electronically, into my bank account. The house payment was automatically withdrawn. There wasn't a lot left. I had to work for Nona, house share or become rich and famous.

I preferred the latter. My experiences with house sharing had not been sublime.


I was fond of this house because it was older than I. It had been built in 1915 when this section of Seattle had been settled by Italians. One of my neighbors was an older woman with that background. Another had, years ago, fled with her husband, from Greece to avoid being an un-fortunate part of a purge. My next door neighbor to the north was a black American. All were accepted as part of our community including me.

The lady from Greece had told me that my house and the one south of it were built by relatives. Between them, they had shared a steep driveway so narrow cars today can't use it. Remembering how my family had helped push our Buick up Colorado mountains in the late twenties, I wondered how early autos had made it up that incline.

My little house was a sturdy, no nonsense dwelling with a full basement. The place was sacred because of the tree.

At some time, a deck had been built. One could come out the back door and walk across a little porch on to it. A rural-looking fence surrounded the structure. There was a weeping cedar reaching high into the sky. Because the lot was on a hill, the back of the deck was eight or nine feet from the ground. The northeast corner seemed to nestle into the cedar. Out there I felt as if I was in a tree house. Below, was a short block down to busy Rainier Avenue and places of commerce. Beyond, residences clung to a hill going up and away to form the valley. If I owned all I could survey from my deck, I would be rich, indeed.

I was rich. Although I still owed half of the value of the property, in the King county court house, it was listed as mine. I didn't need the responsibility of all I could see from my back door. I needed to organize the stuff inside my home.

When I tired of going through papers, I could come out into my tree house. Often I ate out there. It was my favorite place for a picnic.

I meditated there. The shaggy cedar suggested to me, the bearded figure some thought of as God. The wind moved through the lacy boughs like a holy spirit. This was my special sacred space.

## Chapter II
## The Spirit Of Washington

As I get older, I find it harder to remember what I have actually experienced or what I have seen on TV, in the movies or read about.

In the Spring of 1992, a flyer in my mail box had proclaimed there was to be a unveiling of a work of art, behind the library, just a few blocks from where I lived.

I couldn't remember being at such an affair, so I walked to the rolling grassy area behind the Columbia Library. In South Seattle an unveiling at nine on a Saturday morning didn't attract a large crowd even though the mayor of our city was to be there.

When I arrived, I found something about ten feet high wrapped in a blue plastic tarp. Rope spiraled down and around from the top. The sculptor, Marvin Oliver, was there.

I almost wrote, "He was a Native American". His ancestors had discovered this country long before Amerigo Vespucci had found the mouth of the Amazon in 1499. I have no idea how Amerigo managed to get the Americas named after him. He was a navigator. This country is still trying to navigate a peaceful course for the world.... What's in a name? What we put into it.

I couldn't call Mr. Oliver an Indian. That name is a mistake. Columbus didn't know where he was.

We knew where we were that Saturday morning, in Columbia City. I wondered how Mr. Oliver's work had been selected. I had attended several meetings of a group trying to lure artists to Rainier Valley. Rents were less high for studios and apartments. I had gotten the impression that although they hoped to work together to promote the arts, creative egos seemed to pull them apart. Each one wanted his or her talent to be recognized. In this highly competitive atmosphere there seemed to be little genuine admiration for the accomplishments of the others.

I was anxious to see what was under the tarp. The people were congratulating the sculptor. The work was entitled *The Spirit of Washington*. What would the man's impression of that be?

There were speakers from various parts of southeast Seattle. That is made up of areas with names. Mt. Baker and Seward Park are close to Lake Washington. Some homes there are the Up of upper mobility. Beacon Hill boasts of a golf course, places of commerce and residences of various values. Since borders are not well defined, I live close to, if not in Columbia City.

We paler folks are out numbered in some areas. The color of people is not usually important to me, but attitudes are. Those who believe they have a right to cut off drivers in traffic and toss litter for others to pick up, because their ancestors had been slaves, puzzle me.

They call themselves African Americans but they'd be about as at home in Africa as I would be in Ireland or Wales or England.

Sometimes I visualize the young men who congregate next door, driving their customized cars that weirdly dip and sag, down a dusty African road. Who would they talk to on their cellular phones?

They didn't choose to come here? Most of our forebearers didn't want to leave where they were. They simply couldn't stay where they lived.

I'm glad I was born in this country. Some things need fixing. Some things don't.

We need to deal with our prejudices.

I have an acquaintance. She is an attractive brown. She claims that her mother raised her to love everybody. One day she came into Nona's apartment. She was madder than the proverbial wet hen.

"I just found out that I had a great, great, great grandfather that was Irish. Can you believe that?"

"I always knew we were sisters," I grinned.

"Oh," she said in disgust. "I can't believe it."

She stewed for ten or fifteen minutes about her dreadful discovery.

Finally, I said, "You're not prejudiced?"

She said with indignation, "Of course not..."


The mayor of Seattle is black. He is fond of the southeast part of our city. I believe he lived there years ago. He was the last speaker that Saturday morning. He urged us to take pride in our community.

Then he asked all of the children to join him. He took hold of the rope at the bottom of the tarp covered figure. Around and around he went like the Pied Piper with the small ones following. They were shades of brown, red, yellow and pink. They represented all of the children of the world.

When the tarp fell away, there was a dorsal fin of an orca, symbol of the sea, coming out of a rock, the earth. The round head of an early American figure etched into the dorsal fin was opaque resembling a full moon. There were earth, sea and sky. It was the Spirit of Washington. Another sacred space.

# Chapter III
# Martin Luther King

One sacred space should have been discovered by me long before it was. The address of Center Park is 2121 26th Avenue South. Taxi drivers, pizza deliverers, case workers, friends etc. find this confusing. 26th Avenue doesn't exist. Some place north or south it does, but if it came through it would be right in front of the building in which Nona lives. Instead, there is just a turn-around for the Center Park bus and other vehicles. One must turn into Center Park from Martin Luther King Way.

The inside tennis courts are on the other side of this busy thoroughfare. Across Walker street from the courts is the Martin Luther King memorial.

We had watched it being built. In the center of a reflecting pool was a black marble structure that signified Dr. King's struggle for the equality for all. The marble slabs were from Africa, put together in such a way that there were plateaus. It was a steep mountain. It was a waterfall.

The black marble was beautiful. I didn't understand why stainless steel was wrapped around it. They lost me when strange squiggles of bronze were attached. How were they symbolic? They resembled letters of an alien alphabet.

The Martin Luther King Monument stood across a street and an avenue from Center Park. Nona and I hadn't gone any nearer.

Then one day, coming back to Nona's, I drove by the memorial and turned left onto Walker Street. As my vehicle rolled down the hill towards the lot in which I parked, it occurred to me that I should go over there. What had I been waiting for?


After dinner I said, "Nona I'm going over to the King memorial. Want to come?"

She did.

When Nona is in her electric wheel chair, driving on her own, she often panics when there's traffic. Walker was no challenge, but the light allowed little time for us to cross Martin Luther King Way. We made it.

At the time, the approach to the reflecting pool was a gravel path. Nona made that, too. Around this pool were metal plaques. Each offered information concerning facts of Rev. King's life. We were impressed. There was a wall. On it were quotations from Martin L King's speeches. At that time of the day the sun reflected on the raised letters. They glowed. I read:

"I HAVE THE AUDACITY TO BELIEVE
THAT PEOPLE EVERYWHERE
CAN HAVE THREE MEALS A DAY
FOR THEIR BODIES, EDUCATION AND
CULTURE FOR THEIR MINDS AND
DIGNITY, EQUALITY, AND FREEDOM
FOR THEIR SPIRITS. I BELIEVE
THAT WHAT SELF CENTERED MEN
HAVE TORN DOWN; OTHER CENTERED
MEN CAN BUILD UP."

The man had believed as I did. There was in the human heart, a love that could unite us all....

He had been slain.

I read on a large plaque that Center Park had been a contributor. The memorial had been built by donations. There was also the information that Robert W. Kelly, a nationally known Seattle sculptor, had created the symbolic mountain, "difficult and perilous to climb, yet interspersed with plateaus of rest and reflection. Stainless steel banding provides strength; falling water, life force". The marble was from Zimbabwe.

Robert Kelly had died in an accident in April, 1989. This work had been dedicated November 16, 1991. As I pondered the strangeness that both men were dead, I turned toward the pool.

Something that was not alive was floating out by the mountain. It looked like a large black bird. A crow.

Had the creature bumped into the marble and fallen into the water? I was afraid not.

Crows were not lovely alive. This one was ominous in death. I joined Nona reading other plaques. I wasn't about to wade out into the middle of the pool to remove the offensive bird.

When I looked back, the thing had floated to edge of the pool. Before I uttered the words, I knew the answer, "Why me?"

How would I get this large dead thing out of this sacred place?

There were refuse cans with rounded lids. I shuddered as I said to Nona, "This thing doesn't belong here."

With one of the lids, I scooped the crow out of the water. I carried it to the can and dumped it in.

Why had it been there?

# Chapter IV
## The Symbol


It was a miracle. I found the onyx figure when I needed inspiration. My life was at a low. It gave me a high.

I could not imagine how planners could have been convinced to construct a building around an immense symbol of peace. To walk through the door of that City Hall/County Court House in Saint Paul, Minnesota was like coming into a temple. Here the broken and confused could come to seek justice with this soaring figure promising peace.

The statue couldn't soar. It weighed sixty tons, but it seemed to rise like the smoke of the ceremonial fire of the smaller figures gather below.

Carl Mills, a Swedish sculptor, had designed the symbol of world peace from a memory of a Native American ceremony that he had witnessed in Ponca City, Oklahoma in 1929. The walls of Blue Belgian marble, which seemed more black, were lighted to complete the inspirational setting.

I had always loved Native Americans. As a child of six, I spent many hours dressed as an Indian. I can't remember how I came to have the costume and it never entered my mind that gender disqualified me from wearing it. I was an Indian chief. In my imagination, I walked through the forest without snapping a twig. I killed only what I needed to eat and wear. I respected the animal that gave a life for my needs. I felt nearness to the earth and the Great Spirit.

Years later when I came into the temple-like place in St. Paul, I felt again, a oneness with this great figure. He had a feathered headdress far more magnificent than mine had been. In one hand, he held a gigantic pipe of peace. With the other, he offered a greeting.

How had Carl Mills created the design in plaster that touched my soul? How had all the problems been overcome so that onyx came from Pedrara, Mexico by oxcart, boat and rail to St. Paul? How had Giovanni Garatti and nineteen craftsmen carved and put together almost one hundred blocks of this beautiful material to create the largest onyx figure in the world? The massive native seemed to soar to the height of 36 feet. It wasn't enough for it to just be there. In one and a half hours it rotated 132 degrees.

Even though it was a symbol of world peace, I felt so akin to this creation and it gave me so much serenity, I felt it had been put there just for me. It is rare to feel that way about a work of art.

Though I felt it was for me, I knew it drew others to feel as I did. I was glad. One person, alone, can not bring about world peace. It will take all of us. This temple-like place did not welcome some and exclude others.

I marveled again that this glorious tribute to peace, stood in a building where people came to end disputes. God can do wonders working with people.

Almost half a century had gone by since I first discovered this sacred place. It was more beautiful than I remembered. I viewed it from several levels. I found a woman sitting at a desk.

"This is my favorite piece of sculpture," I said.

"I'm glad," she said. "Since you feel that way, let me give you a postcard and a brochure. We've just been through a lot of controversy."

Controversy? How could that be? I didn't ask. I said, "I don't remember seeing the figure reflected in the ceiling. Are the mirrors new?"

"No, people used to smoke in this building so the mirrors up there didn't reflect. "

That was something to ponder. The Native Americans had introduced tobacco to the world. The world had abused it.

I couldn't remember where I had read a Native American's apology for what tobacco had done to us and a reminder of what the white man's firewater had done to Native Americans. Would that we had only good things to share.

I went down to the ground floor to say a reluctant farewell to the inspiring figure.

"Controversy?" I whispered. "How could anyone stand here and think about anything but peace?"

I remembered the first time I had entered this building. Having grown up with a Bible thumping father/preacher, I had to put aside an idea that I was being moved by something pagan. I had not yet decided that all gods were one God.

Humankind needs one very large God....

After all these years, had the conservative Christians with their negative thinking, gotten around to the god of peace?

Later that evening, I was with a son and a daughter. "What controversy has there been about my onyx statue?"

"The Native Americans don't have a god of peace," said Susan.

"The Native Americans objected?"

"Well," said she, "What did some Swede know about American Indians?"

That is what is the matter with the world. Everybody says, "You don't understand." So we stop trying. If Carl Mills was so inspired by a Native American ceremony that he began the creation of something that so inspired me and many others, how could anyone object?

I don't understand why people acquiring freedom start fighting wars over injustices that occurred hundreds of years before. Why can't they let go? What joy do they get from being hateful?

What joy do people in this country get out of insisting they are superior to others. Everyone on this small planet should be concerned about rights for all.

That, to me, was for what the tall onyx figure stood. Inspiration from Sweden, onyx from Mexico, Belgium marble, the creative work of an Italian, the stylizing of a Native American all made a true symbol of world peace.

When I came back to Seattle, I said to a relative, "How could Indians go through a forest so quietly? When I step on twigs they always snap."

"Maybe, they didn't step on them...."

Could there be such a simple solution to all of our problems?

# Chapter V
## Wylanding

In August, 1994, I felt that Seattle would help to save the world. One city, as one person, can make a difference. Positive or negative.

It was Monday, August sixteenth. My granddaughter called me at Nona's. "Wyland is going to be at Northgate Saturday afternoon. I can't go. Maybe Carolyn could."

Wyland. He was probably here to do a book signing. How could he stand to come to Seattle after what had happened to his Whaling Wall on the Edgewater Inn?

For over ten years, I had had a small poster of the first Whaling Wall hanging in my house. Wyland painted whales. Dolphins are the smallest of them. I'd be at the signing on Saturday.

Then on Wednesday, Channel 5's "Evening

Magazine", showed Wyland at work. He had forgiven Seattle for allowing his art to be painted over. He was here to do a new Whaling Wall.

I couldn't believe it.

With great joy, I drove my Dolphin camper to 2224 - 8th Avenue. After fighting a number of one way streets, I found that address. In a small tent gallery, set up in a parking lot, someone told me that Wyland would do two walls. The person thought that Wyland might still be at work. The wall on the other end of the Quality Inn was almost finished. When I walked around the building, there was a life-size orca breaching up into a sunset.

The artist was not to be seen.

Wyland, he uses only one name, usually paints with blues. Here were yellows and oranges. Seattle did indeed have a Whaling Wall again.

I felt like jumping for joy like the orca, but I couldn't.

I walked back to the tent gallery and was told that tomorrow, Thursday, Wyland would begin the second wall. I would be there.

Nona wanted to go with me, of course. In record time, she was out of bed, dressed and in her wheel chair. We left Center Park well before noon.

Parking in the area was not the problem that I expected.

Wyland was slow getting started that morning. The day before two men, repairing the ceiling of the Kingdome had fallen to their deaths. Wyland is no down-to-earth artist. The scaffolding faced a large primed square, towering above us, glaring in the sun. I would not have wanted to go up there.

I am a seeker of shade. There was none in that parking lot. It was Hawaiian weather. Wyland is now a resident of that state. I wished he had brought a palm tree.

We waited. Despite sun screen, Nona's nose was reddening. There was a spot of shade over by the stage that had been set up by a whaling museum. I pushed Nona over there. We waited.

Wyland arrived. He greeted everyone. He signed a brochure for Nona and other things for others.

Eventually he poured paint into a large plastic bucket and then back into the first container. He mixed a green-blue liquid. This was like his usual colors.

We looked up at the large off-white square of wall that reflected heat back at us. Although I wouldn't want to go up there, I wished Wyland would. Nona wanted to see the first strokes that would begin to turn that empty surface into a Whaling Wall. So did I.

There were other painters of whales and dolphins, but this man was in the *Guinness Book Of World Records*. He had painted the largest mural in the world. In Long Beach, California, near the Queen Mary and the Spruce Goose, bullets had flown over his head as he put life-size sea creatures around a convention center. It had been at the time of the riots after the Rodney King verdict.

I wondered how many guardian angels it took to keep Wyland alive....

Any blank wall is a challenge to him. He almost magically turns one into a plea to save the whales he loves.

Finally, he was up there on the scaffolding. Half way up the seven story building, the flimsy looking outdoor elongated elevator paused.

Wyland tested the spray gun. He held it toward the wall. With several mighty motions, he had created land. With small perpendicular movements, he suggested trees.

Having seen the wall's beginning I reluctantly took Nona out of the blazing sun and home. I was feeling parched, but I knew I would return the following day to wall watch.

It was great. I had the feeling that, somehow, a vacation had come to me. I would have traveled to Hawaii to watch Wyland do a wall. He had come here.

In a book I bought, Wyland describes himself as "outgoing and sort of hyper". A good description. He's much more. Unique. One of a kind. Dedicated.

On Friday, when I got to Eighth and Blanchard, on the wall fingers of land were separated by mist. The water below looked so real that I expected one of Wyland's creatures to suddenly splash up into view.

Although I would have liked dolphins, Wyland painted more orcas. On this 8 Murals, 8 Cities, in 8 Weeks West Coast Tour, he was doing whales indigenous to each region. There are dolphins in Puget Sound and Harbor porpoises.... orcas are the largest dolphins. They are a little too large for me.

I bought a poster of his painting, "Dolphin Serenity". I wished I could afford a piece of sculpture. It was a good wish. I have to be careful. I had stood in his gallery on the North Shore of Oahu in 1993 wishing I could meet Wyland. Here he was.

When he began work, he ghosted in outlines of orcas. He made them seem to be coming out of the water that he had painted the day before. He was awesome to watch. I had brought my banana tree umbrella to provide my shade, but after poking some person standing behind me, I went back to the museum area. The man was there from Friday Harbor. He had created large pieces of a puzzle. He encouraged children to put them together to make a whale's tail. The man seemed as dedicated to whales as Wyland.

I kept wanting to call Wyland Whaleland. His name is pronounced Whyland. He painted the sea!

While on the other side of the building, the orca leapt from the water, on this side, a pod of those whales would swim peacefully. I wondered how this man could come back to his chalky outlines and fill them. The scaffold swayed gently back and forth sideways before the wall. From each end, ropes went out over the heads of those who watched. The ropes were held by members of Team Wyland. This arrangement couldn't stop all of the motion. How could he overcome the swaying and paint where he wished? Even with his God-given talent, he had to have the help of angels. I watched as long as I could take the glare and the heat.

On Saturday, I had told my friend, Carolyn, I'd meet her at Northgate at one thirty. It wasn't exactly on the way, but I went by the Wyland walls. The whales were there. One had a cloud of mist coming from the blow hole. Another dripped water from a dorsal fin. All of the whales were painted over half submerged.

Later Wyland told us from his painting perch, that dorsal fins identified individual whales. The markings here were the identifications of actual orcas in the vicinity.

As I watched that Saturday morning, Wyland was having a conference, up on the scaffolding, with the Friday Harbor whale museum man. At first it seemed like an argument. Then, I decided they were working out details of two more whales in the lower right corner. A mother and off spring.

Wyland announced, a little later, that pair was in memory of two orcas who had died in captivity.

The scaffolding was not only a place to paint. Wyland used it as a stage. He wasn't the kind of artist who hid himself in a studio. Perhaps there were times he did that, but he seemed comfortable performing, educating and clowning. He loved what he was doing, but I couldn't help wondering how tired he must be. Creating such large murals had to be physically taxing.

He came down to sign whatever people had. A long line had formed at his table. I joined them. When it was my turn, it was getting late.

I asked, "Are you going to make the two o'clock thing at Northgate?"

"Is it Northgate?"

"Yeah," I laughed, "Northgate. See you there."

I had lunch at a place where I could watch for Carolyn. We were to meet by the totem pole. I finished eating and went to sit on a bench outside. Carolyn arrived.

"Have you seen the walls?" I asked.

"Not yet."

We found Natural Wonders. Carolyn knew where the place was. It is a favorite shop of hers and Nona's. I live in Rainier Valley and don't shop this far north, often. The Center Park bus takes Nona to Northgate about once a month. Unfortunately, the bus had gone to South Center this week. Nona has a weekend aide.

I went to my camper to get the things that I wanted signed. *The* Whaling Wall poster was long and narrow. I didn't want to roll it. As we stood in line with enthusiastic Wyland fans, I had a difficult time holding the poster, the book and calendar. We are constructed with remarkable arms and hands to carry many different-shaped things, yet I have envied the dolphin. The mammal seems to have no need to be burdened with things. Today, I didn't envy the sea creatures. There was something exciting about meeting unusual people and acquiring a signature. Some claim that dolphins had once lived on land and gave up the use of their hands when they returned to the sea. We know so little about whales in the oceans. Maybe Wyland knows.

The lady, just behind us in line, thought Carolyn was my daughter. she could have been. She's about five years older than Wyland.

The woman wanted me to take a picture of her with the artist. She bribed me with, "I'll take a picture of you and mail it to you.”

“Carolyn is better at that than I am,” I said. “She could be in the picture with me.”

Sometime ago, I had, dolphin-like, unburdened myself of carrying a camera. I had read somewhere that the Japanese carefully observed a scene and kept it in their memories. Now the tourist from Japan doesn’t trust the memory. I like the non-camera idea, anyway.

When it was my turn, Wyland said of the poster I placed before him, “This is an old one. “ The letters read The Whaling Wall. It was, indeed, a poster of Wyland’s first wall.

I bought it years before not because of the big whale in the middle or, the little white figure of Wyland, but because there were dolphins at each end. My Wyland connection had started ten years before.

Carolyn was trying to get a picture with Wyland and I on opposite sides of the table. I walked around and beside him, I put my arm around his shoulder. It seemed lake the natural thing to do.

“Ooops,” I said, “am I harassing you?”

He may have thought that I was serious. “Not at all.” he said.

Maybe, long ago, dolphin society had reached the place where touching was suspect. Could that be why they gave up their hands? Was it they simply needed fins more?

I had read his book. We discussed it in a few sentences. Carolyn had bought a copy of a Wyland painting. He signed that. To simplify, Wyland signed only “Wyland 1994”. That eliminated misspelled names, etc.

“You know who you are,” he said.

The woman took Carolyn’s picture and Carolyn took one of her.

On our way to our cars, I said, "Have you been to the walls?"

"No, I'll go later."

"Come on. Go now. I want to show them to you. They're awesome."

We met in the parking lot at Eighth and Blanchard. She was awed.

"I don't know how he does it," I said. "He claims he sees a wall in his mind. How he gets it up there is miraculous. Come see the sunset. It can be seen from the Space Needle."

We went around the building. Now she was so impressed, she didn't want to go home....

Sunday, after church, I was, again, at the wall. Wyland was on the scaffolding but he wasn't painting. He had some of his smaller work up there with him and there was a camera on a small crane.

Later Tiffany, my grand daughter, said, "You were on national TV. You walked right in front of the camera. You had on one of your muu muus. You looked like a Wyland whale. "

"Thanks," I laughed. I had remembered that in line on Saturday it was rumored that Wyland would sell his book and other things on television. It was a mystery how I could have walked in front of a camera taping Wyland half way up a wall.

The artist who acted the salesman, now came down to act the celebrity. There was a long line of us seeking his signature. This time, I had a book for Nona's birthday and my poster of "Dolphin Serenity". I cared only a little that his signing made an object more valuable. I sought the brief contact with this person who was saving the world in his unique way.

"You really do like dolphins," he said.

"You better believe it," I laughed. "Couldn't you hide one behind that billboard up there."

There was a billboard in front of the lower left corner of the wall on this end of the building. A petition to have it removed, was circulating. I had signed it.

He had remembered that I liked dolphins....


A rumor went around that when Wyland went back up to paint, he would put an eagle into the mural. I don't like eagles. Those talons ruthlessly grab too many little animals. The eagle gobbles up many defenseless creatures. I think that it is unfortunate that the eagle is the symbol of the United States.... I would prefer a bird who consumed insects.

I like Wyland's eagle. He doesn't look hungry. Carolyn suddenly appeared in the crowd. She was there when Wyland painted the eagle.

"I don't know what I'm going to do about tomorrow," I said to her. "The dedication is at noon. Maybe we won't go swimming "

"Lonnie will be disappointed."

My friend, Lonnie, liked my sense of humor or the lack of sense in my humor. We played catch in the YW pool Monday mornings and laughed at almost anything. Remember the Disney movie about laughing places? The pool was Lonnie's. She had told Carolyn that it wasn't the same when I wasn't there.

"Hmmm," I said, "if we didn't have lunch, maybe Nona and I could make it down here. "

Nona didn't use her electric wheelchair when we went swimming. One false move and it might go into the pool.

With batteries and all, the chair is heavy and it isn't supposed to get that wet.

Nona panics when there's traffic, so there was no way we could get that far, fast enough if she was in her battery-powered conveyance. Seattle buses have lifts, but we would have to go down a dangerously steep hill to catch one.

I decided to push my friend in her manual wheelchair from Seneca to Blanchard. University, Union, Pike, Pine, Stewart, Virginia, Lenora and Westlake streets were all in between. We'd have to get from Fifth to Eighth Avenue as well. It would be about a mile—fairly flat. I'd be seventy-three in November. I knew younger women who couldn't push a wheelchair that far, that fast. I guess that was one of the reasons, I would. After showering and dressing Nona and myself, I would have about a half hour to make the trip. Coming home we could catch a seven bus at Eighth and Pike.

Huffing and puffing only a little, we arrived at our destination that Monday, just as Governor Lowry walked past. Mayor Rice arrived a little later.

Wyland wore jeans. The red-pink shirt was probably silk. Many different flowers had been gathered for the beautiful lei he had around his neck. No tie.

There was a row of speakers, but the speeches were short and to the point, All of us must be aware that the oceans needed saving...

Two proclamations made August 22, 1994, Wyland Day on the state and city levels.

We followed Wyland around the building. He took Governor Lowry up on the scaffolding with him to sign the wall. When asked to, the governor on that swaying contraption, nervously lettered his name under Wyland 1994, a little too large.

As the crowd went back to the other wall, I heard Wyland laugh, "We'll do this side a little smaller." Up the side of the building went our mayor.

"I don't recall anything like this in my job description," he said. He signed his name petitely.


Already the truck at the curb, decorated with Wyland whales, was being packed. Wyland was due to start a wall at Newport, Oregon the following day. I hated to see him go.

"Happy Wyland Day," I said to the artist.

"He looked at Nona and me. "You've been here a lot this week."

Nona nodded happily.

Seattle had another scared space at 2224 - 8th Avenue.

# Chapter VI
## To Commune With a President

When I talked to the woman who had returned my call, I knew it would be a spiritual thing. One thousand people in the Flag Pavilion would make physical contact almost impossible. Bill Clinton would be in Seattle and I had to be where he was.

I admired the man. There were those who tried to make me believe that he was not to be admired, but who had been through more in the last twenty-one months than Bill Clinton? How had he remained sane?

A governor of a southern state had become leader of the world. That had to be an act of God. There had been too much power and money trying to keep it from happening.

I wondered. If it had been the will of God, why had this young president had to deal with so many natural disasters? Why had he had to cope with the death of his mother?

Was the wonder of finding one's self in such an astonishing position enough to carry a man through all of the world's troubles and his own while many people who had promised to help, now aggressively found fault?

My vote had helped to put him in this position. It was my responsibility to stand behind him even if it cost me one hundred dollars. In another place, the richer Democrats were spending much more to lunch with this man. The money would go to help get an offensively rich Republican out of the Senate and return Democrats to other offices. If only there was some other way to run our government. Too much was spent trying to get votes.

To get where I was going that lovely Sunday morning, October twenty-third, nineteen hundred and ninety four, I'd have to skip church. That didn't bother me too much. I felt God was also with me. My friends at Central Lutheran would miss me only a little.

I started out in plenty of time. I took a bus downtown, walked over to Westlake Center and found that the monorail had temporarily broken down. Starting to walk to Seattle Center, I found myself in a crowd of "Gorton's Gotta Go" sign carriers, being held back by police and yellow tape.

"I've never seen a presidential caravan before," said a young man.

I looked and there was Bill Clinton waving from the back seat of a large dark car. I didn't know how long it would be before I would see him again.


When I found Blanchard Street, I turned right. The Center was straight ahead, but Wyland's Whaling Walls were on Eighth Avenue. The orcas drew me like a magnet.

It was getting late. If the monorail had been working, I would be at the Flag Pavilion by now. I forgot the Democrats were providing light refreshments. I stopped at McDonald's to relieve my hunger and other things.

When I reached the pavilion, there was a long line. Some of the queuers had cards in hand. I thought I should have brought a similar one that I had gotten in the mail. It didn't look like a ticket. The line moved slowly. The Gorton's-Gotta-Go people chanted at the bottom of a large slanting grass area where police sat on well-trained horses. Up by the building were blue and white striped tents. I supposed one was will call. After a long wait, a person wanted my ticket.

"Where is will call?" I asked.

"Down there."

"By the protesters? There is no sign saying that this is a ticket holding line."

A friendly policeman let me take a shortcut to the will call booth. The lines down there were shorter. Most everyone was inside now. The prepaid queue moved well.

Ticket finally in hand, I asked a police officer if I had to wait through the line again.

"Yes," he said, "I'm sorry, but they control who gets in."

Back at square one, there was no indication that it was a ticket holding line. For one hundred dollars each, you could do better, Democrats, I muttered.

A person came by. If I had a blue and white card, I could go to the head of the line. I was a Democrat on two levels. My card was blue and white. Through the gate, I found that at the striped tent, each person filled out a form. Anyone donating over two hundred dollars had to make a declaration. I'd stay under that amount. For the first time in my life, I was close.

As I expected, we went through a metal detector.

Once inside, we stood. In the back of the room, I was surrounded by people. I could see no table for light refreshments. Behind all of us were representatives from all sorts of national news sources. Up front there was a stage. To one side, local channels had equipment.

We stood...

People are better at sitting.

One woman pushed through the crowd. She must have begun to stand before I had. Her face was white. She seemed desperate to get outside.

At my age, I could easily slump to the floor. I hadn't come for that. I had come to send good vibrations to my president. That would be more easily done if I remained upright.


I thought of another gathering in St. Paul, Minnesota. They called it a bean feed. The Democrats were a people party. They offered for very little, plates of beans to thousands. The auditorium was huge. Only Republicans would charge one hundred dollars a plate. The president had been Truman. "Give 'em hell, Harry."

He had.

Now, I had paid one hundred dollars to stand. Inflation? I guess. Those lunching with Bill Clinton had paid much more. Later I heard that to have an autographed picture taken with Bill one donated five thousand. What were the Republicans charging these days?

Maybe like Gorton, they all had millions to spend.

A tall older man offered to stand behind me. He pointed out that I could see the podium if heads stayed right where they were. That was unlikely. Another tall man offered to stand behind so those shorter, could see. Democrats were nice people.

Shortly after one o'clock, two young women entertained us briefly. When they left the stage, there was nothing except a great many people standing.

At least I was inside. One year in Seattle, I had stood in a cold rain waiting for Dukakis. His plane had come in during our worst afternoon traffic. Poor planning. He lost the election. I hadn't paid to stand in the rain. Luckily, it hadn't even cost me a cold.

I wished they would tell us where Bill Clinton was—when he would get here. I guessed they hadn't run out of rich Democrats wanting autographed pictures.

The conversational hum of the gathering was awesome. I wondered how long it would take for each person to drop quietly to the floor.

A man came out to hang the Presidential Seal on the podium. Everybody cheered. He had a little trouble getting it straight.

"It doesn't matter if it's straight, " said someone.

Yes it did.

We needed to feel more respect. That seal stood for something. It stood for the leader of the greatest country on earth. That leader was only a person like all of us here except that seal made him great. It made him stand for all of us.

People needed to stop dissecting presidents, like helpless frogs, and start praying like crazy that the power most of us believe exists would make a president as great as he needs to be.

Those who had given Bill Clinton a job beyond all jobs liked to complain. Bitch, is what they liked to do. He was only a man. With that seal he wasn't only a man. He represented us all. If we were more evil than good then, truly, heaven help the whole world. If we are more good than evil, then there is hope.

A *Reader's Digest* article said that Bill Clinton tried to do good. That was all we had a right to ask of our leader. There was no manual to tell him how to do that. We all needed to pray for guidance not be discontent. This country is what we make it.

I had come today to send Bill Clinton a message. "Keep on doing good."

In this crush of people, I wouldn't get to shake his hand. I wanted to do more than that. I wanted to touch his soul. Each soul is a part of the soul of this nation. Of the world. The White House needed to be a sacred space to heal the earth.

# Chapter VII
## The Encounter


When I heard that there were dolphins, I said, "Oh, no, I don't want to believe that something more intelligent than I lives in the sea".

I keep wishing for things and getting them. After driving a twenty-six foot motor home thirty thousand miles, I wished for a smaller vehicle that consumed less gas per mile. The day I received a check from my parents' estate, there was an ad in the *Seattle Post-Intelligencer*. I bought a Toyota truck. On back, a camper had been mounted by a company in California. It was a Dolphin camper. The unit was almost new.

What we drive becomes part of our identity. If I was to be associated with a Dolphin camper, I would have to admit the mammal existed. That was in 1979.

I bought books. I collected all sorts of dolphins made from all sorts of materials.

I was impressed by the way the dolphin traveled. No packing bags and lugging them through airports. They just swam.

They went celebrating life. Their jumps for joy were awesome. Their arching in and out of the water like rainbows was amazing.

When I tried to be a dolphin at a masquerade, I almost cried. There was no way, I could move like the creature. They are so graceful.

Money and all of the complications of it are not in their watery world. If humans would leave their sea alone, everything they need is there. They live like we might have lived in the Garden of Eden.

They have no need for clothes. Yet they look great. The genitals are tucked into neat slots on the underside.

They enjoy sex, I learned. It is a celebration. They seem to mate for the moment, not for life.

If one saw two large mammals and one small one, swimming in the ocean, it probably would not be a family as we define the word. The two larger dolphins may well be female. The one, the mother and the other may have helped with the birth. She assists, now, with the care of the baby while the mother does what she needs to do. The small one nurses under water every twenty minutes. That is a neat trick. The baby makes a tube with the tongue and the mother squirts milk into the tongue-tube without any saltwater getting into the small mouth.

Dolphins rest often. They don't sleep for hours as we do. The every twenty minutes schedule for them is not as taxing as it would be for us.

The whole pod is their family The sea is their shelter. No rent or mortgages. The decoration of their world with reefs,  plants and colorful sea creatures has been done by their creator and they constantly seem to be praising that force. Their lives are as streamlined as they are. I would like to be more like them. They have such a good attitude.

At the aquarium in Tacoma, a few years ago, they had a dolphin named Sounder. He would not live in the sea without medication. I hated to believe that these creatures could get sick.

I took my grandchildren to see Sounder. He loved children. He came up to them in the underwater viewing area. Someday, I wanted to be closer than the glass allowed. I started wishing.

In 1994, I bought Wyland's book. It showed him in the water beside a dolphin. The place was a research center in Grassy Key, Florida.

There had been an article in the paper. I had had it thumbtacked over my bed until it turned yellow. There was a dolphin in an Irish sea. People put on wetsuits and went out into a bay. If they were blessed, the dolphin swam with them. It was a healing, spiritual experience. That seemed physically and financially out of my range. I didn't want to chance being chosen by a lottery at some hotel. The dolphin didn't seem to have any choice there.

I called quick information at the library. Suddenly, I had the address and phone number of the Dolphin Research Center. I wrote a letter telling someone that I would like to swim with a dolphin on my seventy-third birthday or close to that date. No reply for several weeks. I dialed the phone number several times. Each time, a busy signal. Then one day, I dialed the number and got to talk to a friendly young woman. She told me that I must call on the first of the month to arrange a swim the following month. On the first of December, if I was lucky, I might be able to make an appointment for a day in January. She said that I should keep dialing. The line would be busy....

I wanted to be close to a dolphin so much, I couldn't imagine it would really happen. With six billion people in the world, why should I get my wish?

I had two Silver Wings coupons that expired at the end of December. Flying to Florida from Seattle would earn as many frequent flyer miles as one could earn in continental United States. Could this be happening?

In the first hour that I called December first, I made an appointment for one P.M. the first Friday the thirteenth of the New Year.

If I bought my plane tickets before December thirty-first, the coupons would not have expired. Things were coming together, but I'd never been to the Florida Keys. I had been assured that I would not have to row out to them. I could rent a car in Miami and drive down. My friend, Carolyn, had a free frequent flyer trip that she needed to use. She would go!

I had been to Florida once before. Orlando. Since Carolyn had friends who lived near Jacksonville, we planned to fly into Miami and out of Jacksonville. We'd drive up the coast after my swim.

I kept thinking, "The best laid plans of mice and woman...." This thing that I had wanted so much for so long couldn't be coming about so easily. We'd miss our connection in Washington, D. C. There would be a hurricane.

I had told others that worrying was like living a disaster that would probably never happen, but I couldn't stop fretting.


On January 12th, 1995, I knew that things should be all right while I was gone. Carolyn and I got to the airport easily on the city bus. The takeoff was delayed, but for only a half hour. I had a window seat. Finally, I could sit back and enjoy flying across the nation. I keep forgetting, between trips, how much I really love to fly.

In Washington, D.C., I tried to send the powers that are, good vibrations. If I could arrange to swim with dolphins, they should be able to solve the world's problems.

It was a short flight to Miami. We arrived around eight P.M. We were in a hurry to get our car, but the woman in the booth of the company with my reservation tried to upgrade and sell me insurance that I didn't need.

Finally, I said, "We'd like to get going. I want the small car. Carolyn and I will both be drivers. Please, get us out of here."

The Plymouth Sundance was perfect for our needs. I bemoan the fact that there is, again, such demand for large luxury cars. If someone had discovered a way to make millions selling us sun power, we wouldn't be choking the world and destroying the ozone layer.

The woman had reminded me that some of those people now in Washington, D. C. were put there by the most greedy. How can those who believe in "family values", not care what kind of an earth they leave their children and grandchildren? Beware of gunslingers and those who can't find some other use for land than raising tobacco. If they listened to the God they seem to think they own, there would be the right kind of change.

Dolphins live in a more simple environment. Humans would destroy that for greed.


We had no trouble finding the highway that went down the coast of Florida and became the amazing chain of so many keys.

I had made a reservation at Bone Fish Resort. The woman to whom, I had talked, said the room would be held until we got there. Cabin five was waiting for us.

"See," said Carolyn, "I told you Jo and Ruth were praying for you."

"They're good!" I laughed. "We are in Grassy Key...."

The Dolphin Research Center was across the road and a block or two back toward Miami. We had gotten here.

Friday the thirteenth was warm and sunny. I wouldn't need a wet suit for my swim. We were unpleasantly surprised to find that checkout time at the Bone Fish was 10:30 A.M. The place was unique. Right on the water. I had hoped we could have a leisurely morning and that I could shower just before a noon departure.

Finding coffee and muffins at a shop next to the research center, we picnicked beneath the larger than life breaching dolphins. Inside the center, I checked. I had a reservation. All was well.

The gift shop was filled with all sorts of dolphins that I wanted to own. When we asked, we were told that Wyland had a Whaling Wall on a K-Mart in Marathon. We went back to the Bone Fish, I took my shower and we checked out.

Carolyn drove the few miles to Marathon. It was a beautiful Whaling Wall. It had dolphins. Eventually, we had a light lunch and went back to Grassy Key.

There were about a dozen humans that gathered under a shelter. There was talk about who we were and why we were there and about dolphins and the research center. They loved and respected the mammals there. During hurricane Andy, for their protection, they let the dolphins go out to sea. Only one failed to return.

We were briefed about the swim.

During this time Carolyn was on a tour of the place, taking pictures. We joined the tour. At last we went to the water.

Three much younger women and I would share the company of two beautiful dolphins, Aleta and Santini.

"I brought people for you to play with, " said our leader from the research center.

The mammals threw back their heads and greeted us with joyful clicking that resembled laughter.

When the person closest to me slipped into the water, so did I. I don't know how cold the salty sea was, but the temperature shocked my body. I don't usually feel my seventy-three years, but then I felt all of them. I was old and stiff.

What if the dolphins felt my discomfort? What if I had come across the continent to be rejected by the creatures whom I loved? Maybe it was true that dolphins were drawn to humans in distress. After the first plunge the water felt warmer.

I float well. When it was my turn, I managed to get to the assigned spot. I was floating on my back when I felt a knob touch the arch of my left foot and then the same, on my right. I was being pushed through the water by both dolphins.

If a dolphin ever touched my soul, I hadn't thought it would be like this. I wasn't complaining.

We had been taught to communicate with our hands. When I held out my palm, Santini put her head into it. I pulled her gently toward my cheek. I was kissed. Those strange knobs are not soft. Later I was kissed by Aleta.

A hand palm down asked the dolphin permission to rub her back. I had come through the glass like Alice in Wonderland, I was touching a marvelously hard, rubbery body.

A splash from the hand of us humans was returned by a splash of a flipper. If we twisted, they twisted. I loved it when I held out my arms and Aleta reared back out of the water to offer her fins for a double handshake.

Then it was my turn to go out and tread water. I hoped that I could. I did. Soon one dorsal fin came out of the water beside me. Gently, I took hold of it. Another fin was on my other side. Then I was being pulled through the water between two sturdy, streamlined bodies, at great speed....

The young woman at Sealife Park on Oahu had done this. I had wished that someday.... It was over too soon.

Our leader asked if any of us had missed doing anything.

I said, "I didn't get a gift."

"Aleta, get Blanche a present."

Aleta swam swiftly from us, diving deeply. She came back carrying a plant. Gently, I took her offering from her great, smiling mouth.

As I sat there holding my present, someone said, "It's only seaweed...."

# Chapter VIII
## What is so Good about Evil?

For years, I have thought that I would write about that question. I think I'm ready now. I've been through a little hell.

What is evil? In my life, God and angels are very real. I feel that they are with me most of the time. It is hard for me to believe in the extreme ugliness of genuine evil—the total and complete lack of good.

It is so confusing. Now, people in high places scorn do-gooders. Yet, we have an over supply of do-baders. I haven't longed for the second coming, until recently. I'd love to watch the separating of the sheep and the goats....

I should go on record here. I do a little bad. It makes me nauseated when someone says, "She never said an unkind word about anyone." (I've never heard that said about a man.) What was the matter with the woman? Was she an overachiever in the do-gooder department? We should all wear our halos a little crooked. I think the angels do.

I believe, if I believe, I should be joyful. The last month has been frightening. I have been afraid that I might loose the ability to walk. In 1974, I was supposed to do that. I had shattered my pelvis in an accident. God and I worked things out and I've walked for twenty years. I have spent much of that time helping others who cannot walk. I haven't done this because I'm wonderful. I liked to feel needed. It was a comfortable way to earn enough money to exist. It's really not how much you make, it's how you spend it. For instance, a spiritual high costs less than a drug high. It is a lot less dangerous.

I stay five nights a week in an apartment building housing people with disabilities. At times, I've heard that there was drug-dealing here. To my knowledge, I've never seen a drug dealer. I'm sure a person so engaged, has been in an elevator with me or passed by me somewhere, but they are not inclined to proudly identify themselves. Evil people look very much like good people. That is probably because all of us are good and evil.

I think if I were God, when a person became really nasty, the eyes would glow red like in some monster movies. Trying to hook someone on drugs to make a buck, is about as nasty as one can get.

The Golden Rule should be resurrected. It is in every major religion in some form. Only skin-heads and the like treat hate as a religion.

There is some one who hates me. I can't do a thing about it.

This person got it into her head that I stole her favorite black shirt.

If I remember correctly, the shirt had been purchased at Value Village. Someone's donation. One of a kind.

No, she couldn't have lost it at the laundry.

No, she couldn't have had a vivid dream that seemed real.

When I had asked her if she had found the shirt, she glared at me. She was so sure that I had stolen the shirt, she claimed that she had seen me wear it. Was I trying to drive her mad? I had suspected she was trying to do that to me.

So I have an enemy. In her mind, if I would take her favorite shirt, I would be capable of doing anything. Therefore, she has reason to do anything she can to me.

I haven't walked without pain for over a month. It hurt a lot when I slipped in the bathtub, but that injury has almost healed.

This last Christmas, just before I had arranged to swim with dolphins, the daughter of my enemy gave me a gift. When I was a teenager, I had written a song, "Devilish Little Angel". The little figure from the package was no angel. It was a devilish little devil, right off a tarot card. A ceramic figure about seven inches tall. There were two stubby wings. The goat horns were too large at the bottom for the small head. The flesh face was animal. The body resembled a human. Black flowers clung to the creature. It was a work of art, but when I held it, it felt evil. On the back, a hair pin had been embedded before it had been fired. The top offered a loop for hanging. Could I hang this on a wall like a Christless, crossless crucifix? I wrapped it in its tissue and hid it in the box.

The next time I held it, no matter how I tried to laugh at myself, there was a feeling of evil. I had to destroy this thing.

It fought my destruction, seemingly to resist the punishment I gave it. I felt like a fool. I don't burn books or bash works of art. When it was in enough pieces, the feeling of evil went with them down the garbage shute.

Nothing would keep me from swimming with dolphins. Nothing did.

Now, I can't walk. I hobble and hurt. The old injury reacts to change in the weather. We've had more changes than we do most early Springs. It keeps going from sunny and cold to rainy and warm several times a day. Many times a week. My knee is stiff and weak. It threatens to buckle. God, why can't I walk like a normal person?

Is this caused by some tropical virus from Florida waters? Have I had a slight stroke? I'm passed seventy, is it my old injury telling me I'm old, too? Is there, somewhere, a voodoo doll containing fingernail clippings and several well-placed pins?


Gargoyles don't frighten away evil spirits. Well, several encyclopedias that I checked, don't say that they do. I was hoping....

There is a most delightful gargoyle that spits water running west off the Mt. Baker hill. In South Seattle, pedestrian stairs sometimes take the place of a street. The only things that run down Horton, between 37th and 36th Avenues, are people and rain. People also run up. The rain doesn't.

One of my granddaughters claims that there are gargoyles like this in Europe. I have only seen the one in Seattle. It is perfect for here. It is a clever fountain that gathers natural liquid as it dashes down gutters and directs it over the extended tongue of the semi-evil looking creature. I have never gotten a feeling of demon from this bodiless head. I feel a little sorry for him. He's never had a good hair day.

Gargoyles usually spit rain away from walls. That's what they do. They extend out to keep water from seeping into walls.

I've been trying to remember who first introduced me to the friendly gargoyle in South Seattle. He is not easily found in a residential area where all streets do not go through.

Less than a year ago I rediscovered him. I took Nona there one rainy day. She didn't seem impressed, even though rain splashed merrily over the extended tongue.

I thought the evil looking little creatures sometimes placed on roofs of very old, large structures, were also gargoyles. I guess not. Gargoyles and rain go together. These other creatures are supposed to repel evil. I wonder who decided that... Evil is ugly, how can ugliness repel evil?

Could the place of spouting water on South Horton be sacred? I think so.

# Chapter IX
# Heal Thyself

It isn't easy. That is an understatement. I used to laugh about being in my seventies. I didn't feel old. Then I did....

Our bodies, when they work properly, are collections of miracles. At my age, I get a bit angry at young women who are unhappy about minor defects. So there are two inches too many here and not enough there. They should be celebrating their natural firmness. It is as good as it's going to get. We were not created to be nude in *Playboy*.

I believe we were put on this planet to make it a more joyful place. Why do people enslave themselves with all the other stuff?

In 1995, I found, again, how important health was when I had arranged to swim with dolphins at the Research Center in Grassy Key, Florida. Dolphins can be healers, but when I had jumped into the cold Atlantic water to be with them, I may have pulled something. Old is cold without the c. I felt both. I played with the dolphins. Nothing could keep me from doing that. At the end of the session, Aleta and Santini took me for the ride of which I had long dreamed. Nothing could be as exhilarating for me as racing through the water between two streamlined, great, gray bodies as I held on to dorsal fins.

My body went on strike slowly. After the dolphin encounter, my friend and I drove up the coast of Florida and briefly visited with a couple near Jacksonville.

Back home I seemed alright. I went on caring for my disabled friend, Nona. That's what I do to supplement social security. A few friends and relatives puzzled me. I had wanted to touch a dolphin for years, but instead of celebrating with me, they seemed, I guess, envious. They probably had never wanted to swim with dolphins, but I got the feeling that it didn't make everyone happy that I had gotten to do the thing I had most wanted to do.

Why should it be difficult to find joy in the joy of others? We shouldn't just feel happiness when it happens to us. That's sad. It makes one's world so small.

When I fell in the bathtub my friends were very kind to me. They sent cards wishing me well. They felt empathy when I did something that stupid. I may have cracked a rib. I probably bruised things inside. Somehow I crashed down on a bar put on the tub's edge to keep a person from slipping.

I don't go to doctors. Just before my fall I did go to my dentist. He pulled a tooth, we agreed I could do without. My gums were inflamed. Perhaps that inflammation spread through out my body. I don't know. I couldn't move with out pain. An old left side injury flared up. I could hardly walk.

Everyone told me I should see a doctor. I probably should have, but so many of the women I know, spend so much time going to doctors. God, my guardian angels and a number of books on healing have served me well. If I had been advised to take time off from caring for my friend, there was no one else to do it. The job paid so little, but there was enough for my house payment and an occasional trip. I needed the money. I didn't have time or energy if therapy was suggested.

Often doctors did little for my friends. The government should thank me for not using my Medicare the eight years that I've paid into it. Several times I've thought that I would have to use it.

How does self healing work? My kind is based on positive thinking. I've got to believe. I breathe in love and breathe out hate. I can go through the entire Francis of Assisi prayer if I have a copy before me. One must not forget to breathe in the good stuff and out the bad. One can get confused. Try it.

The prayer begins: Make me an instrument of your peace. If everyone was that, it would cure the world. Think of that a moment....

Then slowly breathe out hatred and in love.

Out injury—In pardon

Out doubt—In faith

Out despair—In hope

Out darkness—In light

Out sadness—In joy!

Out the need to be consoled

In the consoling of others.

Out the longing to be understood

In, great understanding.

Out the desperate need to be loved

In, love!

It is in giving (breathing out)

that we receive (breathing in),
It is in pardoning (breathing out)
that we are pardoned  (breathe in).
The final breathing out will be dying.
Our spirit will breathe in eternal life.


Aspirin helps with inflammation. For my stomach's sake I use the coated kind.

I thank God for everything in my body that doesn't cause me pain. I ask that loving force to heal the things that need healing. I stand tall and feel the spirit move through me.

I try to consume fruit, vegetables and herbs that will help. Although my pet theory on diet is not to worry. When Christ commissioned his disciples to take his message to whomever would listen, he said, "Eat what is put before you."

That seems to imply that if we believe, God will see that the food we eat will nourish our bodies and keep us well.

You have to do what's best for you. Don't try to fit into a mold. All of this political correctness is not good. In a free society, we should not be told how or what to think.

I have decided that I will not fight for women's rights because I am a woman. There must be equal rights for everyone. Love heals. Hate doesn't.

When I was young and a male person said something degrading, I let him know with a look or a remark that he had been crude. If a woman has self-worth it shows.

A healthy body is sexy, but sexuality should not be more important than spirituality. To control something that for the procreation of humankind is meant to be out of control, we need spiritual help.

I think, people should have sexual seasons like other animals. The senseless pursuit of sexual pleasure can wear a body out. Isn't what is called lovemaking only lust-making? Real lovemaking recharges. Lust making cheapens the act and drains energy. It can give the doers deadly diseases.

How can a loving God give us the AIDS virus? How can people pervert sex into "getting lucky"?

A union so intimate should be more than that. Life is not one long prowl to find sex partners anymore than it should be one long drunk. We are given wondrous bodies to care for, not to abuse.

Any kind of drug should be taken only when really needed and then in moderation. If life is so dull one has to use alcohol and drugs to make it livable, alcohol and drugs are not going to help much....

The spiritual umbilical cord between a person and the creator should never be severed. Fortunately, if it has been, it can be repaired.

When I passed seventy, I realized the immune system needed a lot of help. It begins shutting down. That's eventually why we die. Death is nothing to be feared. We are born. We take our turn on earth. We die. This mighty spark in us that we call life goes to another plane.

In 1995 I wasn't ready to go. I had unfinished work to do. So I said to the spirit who usually feels close, "If you want me to finish my work, you must give me less pain and more energy. I can't just work and come home and crash. I need to be unencumbered by pain and stiffness."

I felt that I asked for too much. I worked in a building which housed people with disabilities. There were those who, like Helen Keller, had never seen or heard. There were others who could only look forward to getting worse. There is no cure for many diseases. I could not take on all of their troubles. I could feel compassion.

I could not ask for too much. It doesn't seem to work that way. The more I ask, the more I get. I must remember to praise God for the gifts and remind myself that things occur in God's way and time, not mine.

It takes a lot of breathing out and breathing in.

# Chapter X
## Churches

It may seem like a strange question, but how does a church become a sacred space?

I have wondered about that all of my life.

I was born a disappointment to my parents. They had prayed for a boy. They got a second girl. I arrived on a Sunday morning only hours before my father had to preach a sermon in a small Presbyterian church in Lyons, Kansas. How different it would have been if I had been a son. I know. One joined the family when I was five.

Growing up a little, unwanted dreamer wasn't easy. Few things were as they should have been. So it seemed to me. Churches were full of power struggles. Few people in my father's congregations ever even pretended to wear halos.

My father preached that the people were going to hell. After about five years, it was he and his family who were going. Not to hell maybe, but the next congregation was not close to heaven either.

I always wondered, if people couldn't get along in church, where could they?

As a confused child, I sat in those edifices staring at crosses. Why didn't they just put an electric chair up there? In my child-mind, nobody should proudly display a replica of the thing on which man had painfully killed the son of God. There was no one to talk to. My father was either shut in his study or out dealing with the problems of others. I remember my mother and older sister laughing at my questions until I just didn't ask any more.

Then one day, I had gone into the empty church, next door to where we lived. I had wanted to be alone. I looked up at the thing of torture. Suddenly I realized that they hadn't taken the life of Christ. He had given it. The cross was a symbol of the greatest love humankind would ever know.

I was born again.

This time, I was not unwanted. This time, I was a child of God.

I guess my earthly family didn't find me different. I still dreamed over the dishwater until it grew cold and grease floated to the top. This infuriated my mother. When my sister and I were given dish detail together, we fought.

Yet, inside, I knew that I was loved. In the great family of God there were no disappointments. There were no middle children.

These facts and a devotion to Bing Crosby and his romantic music, got me through my teenage years.

I didn't do anything really stupid until I married at age eighteen. Back then, I wanted to save the world and I thought I would feel less stifled out from under my father's thumb. The church unintentionally helped with my escape. There were prayer meetings on Thursday evenings. While my parents were at one of them, I packed up and eloped.

There were a number of people in that small town who knew this was being planned. No one told my parents.

That congregation was nice to me. They sat through my father's tirade, with my new husband and I, the following Sunday. The subject was ungrateful children. Later, the women went against my mother's wishes and held a bridal shower. Somehow, someone persuaded her to attend. It was a last minute decision. She brought as a gift a yellow teapot. I knew she has gotten it free with the purchase of the Lipton product. It had cost her much more than any other gift had cost any other giver. I valued it.

The town was amused that the Presbyterian minister's daughter had eloped while her parents were at prayer meeting. I had not done it to be amusing. Nor had I done it to cause my parents pain. We all have desperate needs for human love.

I wish that I could say that the healing efforts of that congregation had brought the family closer together. That never happened, We went on tolerating each other. It had been such a nice try.

Then after the births of two children, World War II and two more offspring, the six of us were living near the north border of St. Paul, Minnesota. Sometime in the fifties, a man knocked on my door. He wanted to know if I would like to help build a church. A survey had been taken and the conclusion was that a Presbyterian church needed to be built in that area.

If he found one hundred interested people, we would rent a meeting place and go on from there. My family could be charter members. We needed a church home. I and the four children....

It made my husband nervous to go to church. He seemed to be afraid he'd stand up at the wrong time, not be able to follow the service or fall asleep during the sermon.

He felt more comfortable flirting with waitresses in coffee shops. He smoked many cigarettes and drank a lot of coffee. Could that be why he was nervous in church?

That was sad. No doubt other people feel like aliens when they enter churches. It must be difficult to praise God and feel the spirit when one can't relax. We rarely attended church as a complete family.


The one hundred persons were found. We rented an old house for awhile and eventually built a church that grew over the years, too big for a feeling of family. Big is not always better.

During all of this growth, a wonderful minister, whom we had called, helped me through an unwanted divorce. Wasn't marriage supposed to be forever?

Divorces were more uncommon in the early sixties. It was the woman's fault, even if the man walked out. Though I had been president of the Women's Association, I could not become an elder. I was divorced.

I was still a child of God.

It had not been good for the children. There had been fights in the night. I could not believe a relationship could get so ugly.

The man who left, married three other women before he died. He fathered no other children....


People actually left the church when my younger daughter brought two of her black friends to Bible School. Later, when that daughter married a young man from a mixed union, most of the congregation was supportive. The minister was.

In 1966, I sold my house and everything that wouldn't fit into a twenty-six foot motor home and headed for Oregon. My older daughter had married a minister fresh from the seminary where they had met. Their church was in a little village outside Portland.


Eventually, my younger daughter, three of my grandchildren, and I were living in Seattle. It was there that I found Central Lutheran. It is a small congregation of people who try to love one another.

Recently, at Adult Forum, I felt we were doing that. In a discussion of inclusiveness, we were laughing at ourselves. Some times we tried too hard to make everyone feel comfortable. It wasn't, I felt, the words as much as the spirit that would make us feel togetherness.


Central Lutheran was a sacred space....

# Chapter XI
# The Kingdome

The first event I attended in the newly constructed Kingdome was a Billy Grahm gathering. Even so, back then, I didn't consider the gigantic edifice a scared space. I was disappointed that it didn't have a roof that could be opened.

The big, flat, round, gray building crouched on the edge of downtown Seattle, causing traffic jams whenever there was an event. Once, caught in such a tie-up, I observed people pouring out of the place with baseball bats. I marveled that there were no altercations. It might have been then that I got a hint that there was something special about baseball.

When Washington State became one hundred years old, my granddaughter thought they should decorate the dome with that many candles. When Wyland was in Seattle, he had other ideas for sprucing up the rather dismal exterior.

For most of two decades the building was there, but not often a part of my life.

Then came the 1995 baseball season. The strike was not over and the public was angry. There had been no World Series in 1994. The millionaires who owned the ball clubs still had not come to terms with the millionaires who played the game. Finally, there had been a truce....

Ken Griffey Jr. and the others began to play ball. Home games were in the Kingdome. They hadn't been the year before. Pieces of the ceiling had fallen. It had cost an unbelievable amount of money to fix the tiles that our unbelievable amount of rain had loosened. Even then the dome wasn't good enough.

Management wanted a crystal palace with a roof that opened up. If they didn't get it, the Mariners would leave Seattle. Nobody seemed to care very much. The game had lost its enchantment.


I didn't want the Mariners to leave. Ken Griffey, Jr. was the first easily recognized athlete Seattle ever had. The Sonics had their Rain Man and the Seahawks had had stars, but when a sports figure caught my attention, he or she had to be special.

Ken was. With his irrepressible sense of humor and the way he moved, he reminded me of a dolphin. He broke his wrist in May. Although I couldn't bear to watch the replay of his crash into that wall, it was the making of the Mariners. I can only imagine how that happened.

I didn't follow any sport closely except my friend Carolyn's softball team. On Summer Wednesdays, I took disabled Nona to watch the Greenlake Sluggers. Nona, our friends Ruth and Helen, Carolyn's mother and sometimes others, would cheer them on. Carolyn was called Sox when she played softball.

When the Greenlake Sluggers lost, I'd laugh and say, "Oh, come on, Sox. It's only a game."

Of course, to her it wasn't only a game. Ball players expect to win. It's in their blood. The Mariners had found that a losing team didn't excite fans. But that summer things were changing.

In September, three of us wanted to go to a Mariners game. Junior was back. I hoped not too soon. I suggested September twenty-second, fan appreciation day. Sox couldn't make it, so our friend said, "I've seen a couple of games this year. You two go Saturday."

Sox insisted we go early. When we arrived at the Kingdome, a man directing the parking of cars, told us the game was sold out. We looked at each other. Mariners' games were never sold out.... We made our way to the ticket booth. "The game's sold out," the woman confirmed, "but we have tickets for tomorrow." She tried to be tactful as she said to me, "If you're a senior Citizen you could get in tomorrow for three dollars."

Sox said she couldn't go. I said, "Give me the best three dollar seat in the house!"

When she showed me where it would be, I asked, "Do baseballs come up there?"

"Sometimes, they do," she said cheerfully. I think she thought I wanted to catch one. I just didn't want to get hit.

Central Lutheran would have to get along without me. I was going early. I would get my three dollars worth!

Sunday, when we were allowed inside, I bought a magazine with Mr. Griffey's picture grinning from the cover. I got two. One for Sox. Good baseball fans were supposed to know all about players. Who batted what, when and where. I'd never be a "good" baseball fan.

Junior wanted to win a pennant. I guess his father had been on a team that had won a World Series. Wishing

Junior luck, I bought a Griffey pennant. I climbed the ramps up and up and up. On some level I got a hot dog for lunch.

With a little help, I found my seat. It was right on the edge. Just behind the railing. No one could stand up in front of me. Small chance a ball would come up this high.

All that green down below was awesome. It was a vast board with live playing pieces. I sat up there reading about the Mariners. This was almost as much fun as my swim with dolphins. What was happening to me?

When the game started, I did my Griffey watching. I could look into the Seattle dugout. I watched the young man take his place in the outfield. He made catching that little white fast-moving ball look so easy.

I thought we were going to lose the game. Oakland was one ahead. Had been for awhile.

One of the things that had brought me to the dome was a study of human nature. If those of us who wanted good things for the earth, could figure out what made 57,000 people come together, it might be a start.

That Sunday afternoon, that uniting force was winning. Since we were behind, people were beginning to leave.

Suddenly, Tino brought in a team mate and the Mariners won. As we went down the ramps, I chanted with everyone else, "Tino, Tino...."

I never really left the dome. I stayed in spirit. Though I watched on television, I felt I was with the team. There were many of us. We made up a spiritual guardianship. We wanted nothing to harm the Mariners.

I discovered Lou Piniella. Sox said he had been born again. In an interview Lou said, "I'm basically the same person, but there's more humility, more meekness in me now. It's true I'm born again. .... I don't think of myself as a born again Christian, but as a Christian."

His choice of chew was bubble gum. I watched with envy as expanding, pink, air-filled globes came from his lips. Never had one come from mine.

He had other talents. He played the players like a master chessman without forgetting they were people. He let them know where they stood and encouraged them to be all they could be. He had learned from managers I had heard of—Billy Martin and Yogi Berra—and some I hadn't.

In the magazine that I had bought, he said, "In the end a manager has to be himself. He can't be anyone else. A manager is basically there to lead, to steer things, keep things positive and calm as possible and let the kids play."

He did those things and more. I liked who he was. He knew that as we prayed to win, the other team prayed for us to lose.

The Mariners refused to lose.

They suffered through a series with tobacco-chewing Texans.

Randy Johnson who grinned from the Eagle commercials, grimly intimidated batters to strike out. There was a play-off with a California team and before the Mariners could rest up, they flew to an open stadium in the East. When they flew back to the Kingdome; a miracle happened. Junior ran like the wind from first to home behind Joey Cora. We beat the New York Yankees!

When the team jumped onto Junior's back we all cried, "Don't break him. We have games to go."

The commentators had constantly reminded us that one miscalculated pitch could lose a game. It wasn't like softball's lazy arches. The ball could travel ninety miles an hour. The batters were supposed to figure, in a split second, if the small orb coming at them was a fast, breaking, curved or whatever kind of ball and would it cross the plate where it could be hit. This game required men to be excellent. Only God is excellent.

The whole Seattle area fell in love with the Mariners. When they finally lost to Cleveland, we all cried with Joey.

That's when the Kingdome became a sacred space.

Junior, who had grown up in baseball, went to the locker room. Those of us watching felt the pain. The fans didn't leave the dome.

The Indians went to do their celebrating. The Mariner fans stayed on to cheer for Joey, Junior, Jay, Tino, Edgar, Randy, Norm and Lou, every player and staff member. This was unusual for fans of a losing team.

Junior was convinced it was happening and came out. The Unit waved his wonderful arm at the crowd.

Thousands and thousands of people had been united by a special kind of love. Not just those at the dome, but all of us from a very large surrounding area.

I felt there was hope for the world.

# Chapter XII
## Believe

There were those who wondered why a woman in her seventies would travel to an unfamiliar city by herself. I had a mission.

I have a fantastic faith. It takes a whole flock of angels to help me do what I have to do. First an idea bounces around in my brain. After the excitement the Mariners created last fall, I was getting the urge to go to Spring Training.

Now this was strange. I wasn't a sports kind of person, but I wasn't the kind of person most people think of as "a woman in her seventies," either.

Since my marriage had failed thirty-three years ago, and my grandchildren had all grown up, I had had crushes on various celebrities. This fantasy stuff was safe, but rather unsatisfactory. Then I fell in love with an entire baseball team.

I was not alone. If I had a dollar for every person the Mariners had touched in 1995, I could self-publish all of the books I have written and have plenty left over for all sorts of wonderful projects.

They were so young.... Many of the Mariners' coaches, including "Sweet Lou" were about the ages of my children. Ken Griffey, Jr. was younger than my grandchildren. I adopted the whole team.

All "my children" wanted to win the World Series.

When I had visited friends in San Francisco at just the right time, I had been given a free trip to anywhere my favorite airline sent a shuttle. One of those cities was Phoenix. My angels were pushing in that direction.

I made the arrangements. I would have a rented car. There would be a suite. (Not my usual accommodations.) Full breakfasts would be provided. Also, two ball games and after a BBQ, Lou Piniella would lead a chalk talk. The fine print added, "or a member of the staff".

"Could you," I whispered to the force who organizes my angels, "make that Lou?"

In Phoenix, my shiny new red Chevy kept getting lost. I finally found the Fountain Suites Hotel. My suite was the same size as the first floor of my small house in Seattle. There were two TVs, two phones and one me....

I was on a Mariners' mission.

On Saturday, March 9, after a struggle with the Cubs, my team won .

After a well-planned BBQ, Lou Piniella did the chalk talk! He was tanned and mellow. He fielded our questions like the pro that he is. He told us how tough it was going to be to make the cuts he would have to make. It was an awesome responsibility. How could he tell at this point which rookie with coaching might become another Junior or a Randy?

He laughed as he recalled that that very afternoon, one rookie came recommended as a pitcher by members of his staff. The first thing Lou knew the bases were loaded. Then he told us that when he felt a pitcher must be taken from the mound, he was going to have two signs—Yes and No. He'd let the fans decide. If it didn't work out, the fans could boo themselves.

Later, Lou signed my official Spring Training Tour cap. I thanked him for being there. He thanked me for coming.


Sunday, I saw more of Phoenix than I really wanted. As I wandered around, I realized what a remarkable place it was. There were training camps and stadiums all over the area.

The A's clobbered my team, but I knew Lou was giving a large number of players a chance to show what they could do.


Monday, my plane didn't leave until the afternoon. In the morning I went out to hallowed ground. The place were Mariners trod. I watched many hopeful young men tramp by in the familiar blue and white uniforms. My heart ached for those who would be cut.

I went to watch the greats.

I was worried about Junior. He had gotten his wrist to work after the break, but what if that member of that amazing body would not respond in the same way after all of that hardware had been removed. I watched him bat. Not good. Before he walked off with Jay, laughing, I gathered all of the forces that were with me and sent them to surround those remarkable men.

Before my plane touched down in Seattle, Ken Griffey, Jr. had hit a home run....

As I sit here looking at a picture of the World Series trophy, I'm impressed by its beauty. How close can Seattle come this year?

I suggest a new slogan: BELIEVE

# Chapter XIII
## There Is No End

For a day or so, I lost my faith over a penguin. Usually a strong loving force is with me. Just as it should be with everyone. This love is our only hope. It is every where at once—a strong uniting power. We should all be part of it.

I feel guilty when I question this force. Many times in my life, I have been told that if I don't accept God without question, I would be hit by a lightning bolt.

A little education can be a dangerous thing. It was a nature program about penguins that put me in danger of being bolted. My memory isn't the greatest. It never was. The facts may be fuzzy, but I believe it was the largest of the penguins that the commentator described  in detail.

The story went something like this. The species lived most of the time in the coldest part of the world. The females laid eggs, tucked them under the males and went off to warmer climes. For months those poor males hovered together for warmth. They ate nothing. They just stood there keeping an egg warm beneath a special skin flap.

Why would a creator do that to any living thing? I couldn't think of a reproduction plan more unpleasant. I was depressed until I remembered that I wasn't a male penguin. Human females go through nine months of all sorts of discomforts to reproduce. This penguin was a species where the females frolicked in the sea, while the males clustered together keeping themselves and eggs warm in sub-zero weather.

After the incubation period the females came back to release the males to go find food. If the female didn't come back to her male, the egg and its protector perished. It seemed like a plan invented by liberated women.

The males sort of hibernated. Other animals did that. Time must not be the same as it is to humans. It was remarkable that the cold could be endured.

Animals are locked into behavioral patterns. Why do humans have so much freedom? Why do we get into much more trouble?

I'm learning that even dolphins are not as free as I had thought. Scientists claim they are programmed...

It is almost overwhelming to be human. We have too many choices and not enough guidance. There is guidance, but it is too often disregarded.

Humans try to program others. Some try to force other people to pray, their way; buy products not needed; think certain things; do what the would be programmer wants them to do....

When "nature" programs, it is much more effective. Never would a penguin say, if he could, "I'm cold and hungry, let's go where it's warmer and get something to eat."

The force called nature, because humans seem afraid to believe in God, won't allow such behavior. The females never fear that they might come back to a vast snowy area dotted by deserted frozen eggs. Should humans be programmed to be so reliable?

Do you believe that all the other creatures worry about humans becoming extinct? Or are they just doing their things, hoping we will? Are we Jonathon Swift's Yahoos in *Gulliver's Travels*? They created no sacred spaces. They had only the qualities of the worst of us.

I was puzzled by an article in the *TV Guide* the week the story appeared on the small screen. It suggested that in one sequence, people had been blinded by religion. Jesus opened the eyes of the blind.

The Yahoos were subhuman. There was nothing spiritual about them. People who don't think that they believe in God, have instincts to care and share. Most children want to be good and feel badly when they're not. Don't we all like to give good impressions, be heroes, seem helpful?

Yet, there are some to whom nothing is sacred. It is an interesting word. I kept wanting to spell it scared. Put in another r and it's scarred.

I have been looking for spaces, sacred. I disregarded several dictionary definitions until I came to: entitled to reverence.

Reverence: honor or respect felt or shown. If we honored or respected more places and persons, the earth could only become more sacred.

Total lack of respect creates death and destruction. Life is a precious gift. No one has a right to take it from another. No one should needlessly cause another pain.

Those really close to the loving power cannot completely disregard the feelings and beliefs of others, even in an election year. There is an unhappy end for one who calls his/her brother/sister a fool....


Why didn't this power program people like penguins? Then, many things, for which the power is blamed, wouldn't happen.


How can I expect Seattle to save the world? Seattle has had practice. *The Seattle Post-Intelligencer*, our morning newspaper, held a contest. They wanted an identifying symbol.

Jakk Corsaw won by suggesting a circular mural of the world. A three-dimensional globe was created by Pacific Car and Foundry and Electric Products Consolidated in 1948.

Somehow the 18.5 ton structure was hoisted onto the top of the building at Sixth and Wall. It was crowned with an eagle over eighteen feet high. Circling the equator were letters, the capitals, eight feet tall, proclaiming, "It's in the P-I."

When Seattle citizens heard that the paper planned to move to 101 Elliott Avenue West, many wanted to know what would happen to the world.

The P-I acted on the recommendation of a panel of art experts and citizen activists. The symbol would be saved. It was no easy task.

The upper and lower hemispheres were parted, taken down, and refurbished. Eventually all was well. The slogan was lighted and began to turn again on the roof of the new building. "It's in the P-I." It was still in Seattle.


Each time I see the sizable globe secure on top of the newer Post-Intelligencer building, I say softly, "Seattle can save the world...."

# ORDER FORM

Additional copies of *Seattle Sacred Spaces and Other Places to Heal the Earth* may be ordered by writing to:

B. Lees
4016 Letitia Avenue South
Seeattle, Washington 98118

Please make out your check or money order to: B. Lees.
*Thank you.*

Name:_______________________________________

Address:_____________________________________

City, State, Zip:______________________________

copies @ 11.95 each__________

WA residents add 8.2% tax__________

$2.50 shipping/handling__________

Total__________